THE RIGHT COMBINATION

There is only one 4-digit combination in the list below that will unlock this safe. Each of the three clues will help you cross off the combinations that WON'T work.

Clues:

- No digit is repeated within the correct combination.
- Three of the digits in the combination are even numbers.
- One of the digits in the combination is an odd number, and that odd number is less than 7.

6559 1331 9264

8251 2486 1753

2678 4832 6388

Illustrations: Paul Richer

Can you tell what saying is represented by each picture?

A _____

B _____

C _____

D _____

E_____

F_____

G_____

H_____

I_____

Answer on page 33

BEE CAREFUL

These bees are gathering pollen to take back to their hive. If each bee carries away one pollen ball, will there be any pollen left in the flower?

6

Answer on page 33

WHAT'S THE CATCH?

Fishing was good today. Now it's time to check the catch. Each basket is tagged with the weight of the fish inside in pounds and ounces. Help the game warden by determining who's over and who's under the legal limit.

LEGAL LIMIT 144 oz.

8 lbs.

8 lbs. 4 oz.

9 lbs. 3 oz.

10 lbs. 1 oz.

7 lbs. 15 oz.

8 lbs. 10 oz.

Hint on page 32

ON AVERAGE

Brian got to bat three times during the big game. He knocked a single, smacked a double, and walloped a triple. What was the average number of bases Brian scored during the game?

During a skating trial three judges awarded Sylvia the scores of 8, 9, and 10. What was Sylvia's average score?

It took Terri three hours to reach Big Adventure Fun Park. She drove forty miles in the first hour, sixty miles in the second hour, and thirty-two miles during the third hour. What was her average speed in miles per hour?

Illustration: Lindy Burnett

Answer on page 33

Ralph went on a fishing vacation for four days. The first day he caught two fish, the second day he caught one fish, the third day he didn't catch any, and on the fourth, he caught five. What was the average number of fish he caught per day?

Here is Clete's schedule for the number of movies he saw this week.

M	T	W	T	F	S	S
1	2	1	3	2	4	1

What is the average number of movies Clete saw each day during the week?

Hint on page 32

ALL IN A ROW

*E*ach rollicking robot has a numerical feature in common with the others in the same row. For example, the robots in the top row across all have three wheels. Look at the other rows across, down, and diagonally. Can you tell what they have in common?

Hint on page 32

Illustration: Marc Nadel

Answer on page 33

COLOR BY NUMBERS

Use the key at the bottom to find a colorful character.

KEY

1 = Brown
2 = Yellow
3 = Blue
4 = Red
5 = Tan
6 = Gray

Illustration: Rob Sepanak

Answer on page 33

SET UP

Illustration: R. Michael Palan

"Sets" are groups of things that belong together. One set in this illustration is a set of numbers (1, 2, 3). There are at least five other ways that the numbers in

STAN

Answer on page 34

this illustration can be grouped together into sets. Can you help Stacking Stanley organize them? Hint: One of the sets is all of the green numbers.

KATE'S KITCHEN

Kate has guests coming for dinner at 7:30. She plans to prepare the items on these cards. She thinks she has enough ingredients. The question is, if she does one thing after another, does she have enough time to make everything before her guests arrive?

Illustration: Terry Kovalcik

SALAD

1 head of iceburg lettuce
$\frac{1}{2}$ head of romaine lettuce
1 tomato
2 carrots
2 stalks of celery

Prep time: 10 minutes

DESSERT

2 sticks of butter
cake mix
1 cup of milk
eggs
oil

Prep time: 1 hour and 5 minutes

Magic Meat Loaf

5 pounds of ground beef
1 onion
$\frac{1}{2}$ tsp pepper
1 tbsp salt
2 tsp garlic powder
1 can of tomato sauce
1 pound cheddar cheese

Prep time: 40 minutes

GRAVY

1 cube of boullion
1 package of spices
3 tbsp cornstarch
$\frac{1}{2}$ cup water

Prep time: 8 minutes

Vegetables

14 oz. fresh peas
$\frac{1}{2}$ stick butter

Prep time: 14 minutes

Answer on page 34

COUNTDOWN

Start at 33 and count your way down to see something out of this world.

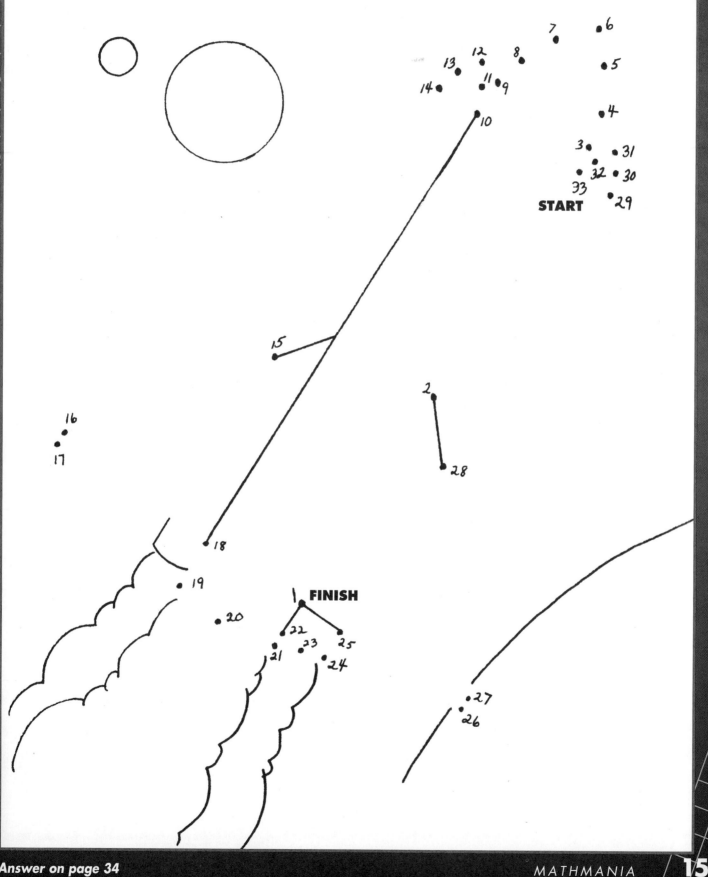

CASTLE CALCULATION

People say there is a secret treasure hidden inside this creepy castle. To find it, you must be a quick thinker as well as a quick runner. Each time you pass one of the wall torches, the secret door either locks or unlocks itself. For example, if you pass a torch and the door unlocks, the very next time

Illustration: Jerry Zimmerman

START

you pass a torch, the door will relock itself. You cannot go back over your path or the door will seal itself for another hundred years. The door is now locked. Can you find a path that will bring you into the library while the secret door is open?

Hint on page 32

HOLD MY PLACE

All aboard! Each vacant window is a placeholder for one of the number passengers underneath that car. Look at the luggage for clues to where each number belongs. Can you put the numbers in the right seats? Hint: Think of the row of windows in each train car as a number in the 100,000s. Under the blue car, the orange passenger "2" is carrying a suitcase labeled "hundred thousands." So orange 2 will sit in the first window of the blue car.

Illustration: Barbara Gray

Answer on page 34

The number accompanying each picture represents a letter in the name of the object. For example, the number three beside the snake means you want the letter A. First, find the letters, then unscramble them to answer the riddle.

3

3

2

1

5

1

1

2

3

4

Hint on page 32

3

Illustration: Jerry Zimmerman

What animal do you get when you cross a pig with a tree?

___ ___ ___ - ___ - ___ ___ ___ ___

TRICK QUESTIONS

Be sure to read each question carefully before you answer.

1 Farmer Brown has three piles of hay in one field, two piles in another field, and four piles of hay in a third. If he moves all the hay together, how many piles will he have?

2 Rocky has been digging all afternoon. He started at noon and by 2:15 he had a hole that was larger than a small car. How long would it take someone to dig half a hole?

Illustration: Scott Peck

3 You are driving a bus. At the first stop, three people get on. At the second stop, one person gets off and three other people get on. At the third stop, four people get off and two people get on. At the fourth stop, one person gets off and no one gets on.

a. How many people, including the driver, are on the bus after the fourth stop?

b. What color are the bus driver's eyes?

Answer on page 34

PRECISE ICE

Hillary is getting ready for another competition. She's been practicing on this design all day. Can you show her how to make the design without crossing or retracing any line?

Illustration: Barbara Gray

Answer on page 34

CANDY COUNTER

Clark has a dollar to spend. He will walk out of this store with 100 pieces of three different kinds of candy. Looking at the costs per piece of candy, can you tell how many pieces of each kind of candy will be in his bag?

Licorice whips: 10 cents

Lollipops: 3 cents

Gum balls: 2 for 1 cent

Illustration: Terri Kovalcik

Answer on page 34

BUY WEEKLY

Jeremy makes $15.00 a week doing lawn maintenance for a neighbor. He also gets $2.00 allowance for each week he does all his chores. He's made a list of some special items he's saving to buy. How many weeks will he have to work in order to get everything on his list?

New bike tires	$37.50
Flash Endipan rookie baseball card	$22.00
Running shorts for Mom	$26.50
Under Thunder's new CD	$14.00
Puzzle book	$5.00
Flea collar for Buddy	$3.00
Surprise pizza for Dad	$11.00

Hint on page 32

Illustration: R. Michael Palan

Answer on page 35

DIGIT DOES IT

That notorious crook, Penny Ante, tried to make off with Bill Buxley's coin collection. But Inspector Digit arrived in time to scare Penny away.

Illustration: John Nez

Answer on page 35

First, decode Penny's note.
(The first line reads "Dear
Inspector Digit.") Then see
if you can help Digit do
what the note says.

$\overline{21}\ \overline{20}\ \overline{24}\ \overline{9}$ $\overline{16}\ \overline{12}\ \overline{8}\ \overline{10}\ \overline{20}\ \overline{22}\ \overline{7}\ \overline{11}\ \overline{9}$ $\overline{21}\ \overline{16}\ \overline{18}\ \overline{16}\ \overline{7}$,

$\overline{7}\ \overline{17}\ \overline{16}\ \overline{8}$ $\overline{13}\ \overline{24}\ \overline{2}$ $\overline{12}\ \overline{11}\ \overline{7}$ $\overline{13}\ \overline{24}\ \overline{15}\ \overline{20}$

$\overline{22}\ \overline{20}\ \overline{12}\ \overline{7}\ \overline{8}$, $\overline{23}\ \overline{6}\ \overline{7}$ $\overline{16}\ \overline{14}\ \overline{14}$, $\overline{18}\ \overline{16}\ \overline{5}\ \overline{20}$

$\overline{2}\ \overline{11}\ \overline{6}$ $\overline{24}$ $\overline{22}\ \overline{17}\ \overline{24}\ \overline{12}\ \overline{22}\ \overline{20}$ $\overline{7}\ \overline{11}$

$\overline{9}\ \overline{20}\ \overline{22}\ \overline{11}\ \overline{5}\ \overline{20}\ \overline{9}$ $\overline{7}\ \overline{17}\ \overline{20}$ $\overline{23}\ \overline{6}\ \overline{3}\ \overline{14}\ \overline{20}\ \overline{2}$

$\overline{19}\ \overline{11}\ \overline{9}\ \overline{7}\ \overline{6}\ \overline{12}\ \overline{20}$. $\overline{20}\ \overline{5}\ \overline{20}\ \overline{12}$ $\overline{7}\ \overline{17}\ \overline{11}\ \overline{6}\ \overline{18}\ \overline{17}$

$\overline{2}\ \overline{11}\ \overline{6}$ $\overline{18}\ \overline{11}\ \overline{7}$ $\overline{17}\ \overline{20}\ \overline{9}\ \overline{20}$ $\overline{16}\ \overline{12}$ $\overline{7}\ \overline{16}\ \overline{13}\ \overline{20}$,

$\overline{21}\ \overline{11}$ $\overline{2}\ \overline{11}\ \overline{6}$ $\overline{7}\ \overline{17}\ \overline{16}\ \overline{12}\ \overline{15}$ $\overline{2}\ \overline{11}\ \overline{6}$

$\overline{22}\ \overline{24}\ \overline{12}$ $\overline{19}\ \overline{16}\ \overline{12}\ \overline{21}$ $\overline{24}\ \overline{14}\ \overline{14}$ $\overline{7}\ \overline{17}\ \overline{20}$

$\overline{17}\ \overline{16}\ \overline{21}\ \overline{21}\ \overline{20}\ \overline{12}$ $\overline{22}\ \overline{11}\ \overline{16}\ \overline{12}\ \overline{8}$?

TRIP THE LIGHT-YEARS FANTASTIC

he crew of the spaceship *Tralfamawindo* is in deep trouble. It has only enough energy pods left to travel 57 light-years. Can you add up

3

6

5

9

4

7

8

9

5

3

6

4

3

2

7

4

5

9

the light-year distances to
see which celestial body
the crew can reach by
going until the fuel dial
reads exactly empty?

Illustration: Scott Peck

FOR GOOD MEASURE

Help our maestro finish transcribing this song. The time signature at the top says there should be four beats in each measure. Use the chart to put in the notes that will keep the beat and make the music sweet. The x in each measure will show you where to add a missing note.

measure

Illustration: Jerry Zimmerman

= eighth notes
2 equal 1 beat

= quarter note
1 beat

= half note
2 beats

= dotted half note
3 beats

= whole note
4 beats

Hint on page 32

Answer on page 35

$E = 5^2$

If you cut out the letter *E* below, then cut the letter along the red lines, you'll have five pieces. See if you can arrange those five pieces to make a perfect square.

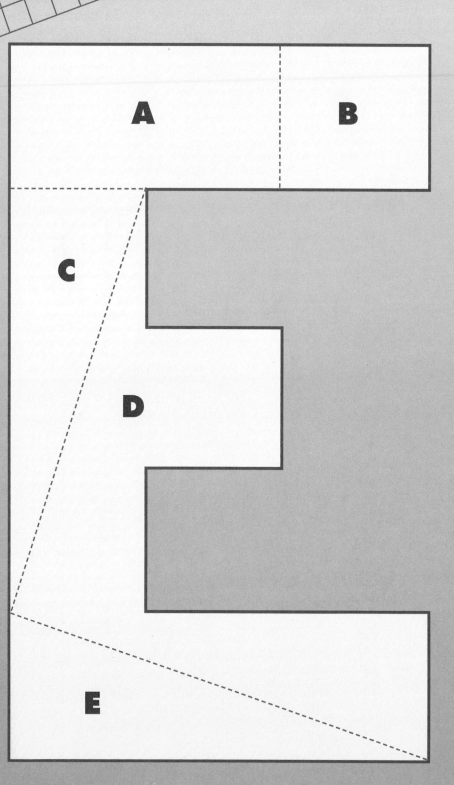

DOMINO THEORY

This is a game of dominoes. In a full set each of the 28 domino tiles has two halves and the dots on each tile equal a pair of numbers: 0 and 0, 0 and 1, and so on up to 6 and 6. Domino halves with the same number of dots are placed next to each other. The red circles on the boards represent half-tiles with no dots. A tile placed with its middle against another has an equal number of dots on each side. The tiles with the X's have already been played. Can you use the rest to fill in this board?

Hint on page 32

Answer on page 35

HINTS AND BRIGHT IDEAS

These hints will help with some of the trickier puzzles.

WHAT'S THE CATCH? (page 7)
To find the weight of each catch, remember there are 16 ounces in a pound.

ON AVERAGE (pages 8–9)
To find the average of anything, add the numbers together and then divide by the number of things you added together. In the first question, Brian got a total of six bases, which you divide by the number of times he got to bat.

ALL IN A ROW (page 10)
Look for the same numbers of things on the different robots.

CASTLE CALCULATION (pages 16–17)
This path shows how to get through a small set of rooms so that the door will be open.

T	T	T	T	T	Gate
Open	Close	Open	Close	Open	

LAUGH LIST (page 19)
When unscrambling the letters, A goes in the first blank.

BUY WEEKLY (page 23)
Add all the prices together to find how much Jeremy needs. Then divide by how much he makes each week.

FOR GOOD MEASURE (page 28)
Each measure should contain notes that add up to a total of four beats. None of the notes you will add will be eighth notes.

DOMINO THEORY (pages 30–31)
Use all 28 possible number combinations. Cross each domino off as you find a place for it. Put tile halves with the same numbers next to one another. If a domino is up against the middle of a second domino, the second has the same number of dots on both halves. Check the 3–3 domino given to start with. Remember that dominoes can be flipped around, so you can place either side against another domino. For example, 2–3 is the number pair for one tile. That domino can be placed against either a 2 or a 3.

ANSWERS

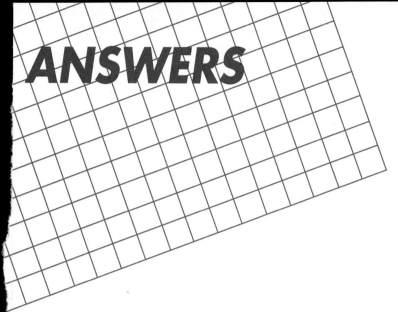

COVER
Pig — $4.00
Safe — $3.60
Ball — $4.35
Fish — $5.60

The fish has the most money.

THE RIGHT COMBINATION (page 3)
4832

REBUS BY THE NUMBERS (pages 4-5)
A. Hole in one
B. Six of one, half dozen of another
C. Behind the eight ball
D. Tea for two
E. Three-way tie
F. Seven seas
G. Nine out of ten
H. High five
I. Four-H

BEE CAREFUL (page 6)
There will be two pollen balls left behind.

WHAT'S THE CATCH? (page 7)
144 ounces (oz.) equals 9 pounds (lbs.). Only the two whose catches are over 9 pounds are over the limit.

ON AVERAGE (pages 8-9)
Brian scored an average of 2 bases per at bat.
(six bases ÷ 3 at bats)

Sylvia's average score was 9.
(27 points ÷ 3 judges)

Terri averaged 44 miles per hour.
(132 miles ÷ three hours)

Ralph caught an average of 2 fish a day.
(8 fish ÷ 4 days)

Clete saw an average of 2 movies each day.
(14 movies ÷ 7 days)

ALL IN A ROW (page 10)

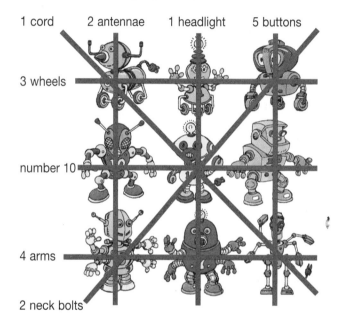

1 cord   2 antennae   1 headlight   5 buttons

3 wheels

number 10

4 arms

2 neck bolts

COLOR BY NUMBERS (page 11)

SET UP (pages 12–13)

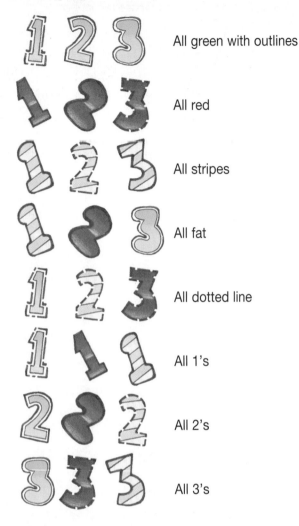

All green with outlines

All red

All stripes

All fat

All dotted line

All 1's

All 2's

All 3's

KATE'S KITCHEN (page 14)

She'll be finished with three minutes to spare.

COUNTDOWN (page 15)

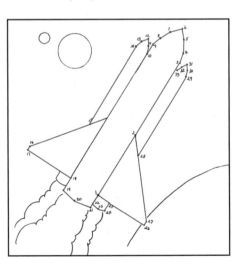

CASTLE CALCULATION (pages 16–17)

HOLD MY PLACE (page 18)
202,019
516,014
987,456

LAUGH LIST (page 19)
What do you get when you cross a pig with a tree?
A PORK-U-PINE

TRICK QUESTIONS (page 20)
1 – If he puts them all together, he'll have one big pile.

2 – You can't dig half a hole. Once you take out even a spoonful of dirt, you've made a hole.

3 – a. Three
    b. You're the bus driver. What color are your eyes?

PRECISE ICE (page 21)

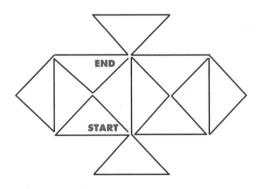

CANDY COUNTER (page 22)
5 whips at 10 cents = .50
1 lollipop at 3 cents = .03
94 gum balls at 2 for 1 cent = .47